Standards

for school media

programs

Prepared by the American Association of School Librarians
and the Department of Audiovisual Instruction
of the National Education Association

in cooperation with representatives of the
American Association of School Administrators
American Institute of Architects
American Personnel and Guidance Association
Association for Childhood Education International
Association for Educational Data Systems
Association for Supervision and Curriculum Development
Association of Chief State School Audio-Visual Officers
Association of Classroom Teachers
Association of School Business Officials
Association of State School Library Supervisors
The Catholic Library Association
Council of Chief State School Officers
Department of Elementary-Kindergarten-Nursery Education, N.E.A.
Department of Elementary School Principals, N.E.A.
Department of Foreign Languages, N.E.A.
Department of Rural Education, N.E.A.
International Reading Association
National Association of Educational Broadcasters
National Association of Independent Schools
National Association of Secondary School Principals
National Catholic Education Association
National Committee for the Support of Public Schools
National Congress of Parents and Teachers
National Council for the Social Studies
National Council of Teachers of English
National Council of Teachers of Mathematics
National Science Teachers Association
National Society for Programmed Instruction

Published by the American Library Association, *Chicago, Illinois*
and the National Education Association, *Washington, D.C.*

1969

This publication can be purchased from the
American Library Association
50 E. Huron St., Chicago, Illinois   60611
or from the
National Education Association
1201 Sixteenth Street N.W., Washington, D.C.   20036

Standard Book Number, American Library Association, 8389-3001-8 (1969)

Library of Congress Catalog Card Number 69-20497

Manufactured in the United States of America

Members of the joint committee*

Miss Elenora C. Alexander (A)
*Director, Instructional
   Materials Services
Independent School District
Houston, Texas*

Dr. James W. Brown (D)
*Dean, Graduate Studies and
   Research
San Jose State College
San Jose, California*

Dr. Richard L. Darling (A)
*Director, Instructional Materials
Montgomery County Public
   Schools
Rockville, Maryland*

Miss Leila A. Doyle (A)
*Library Consultant
School Library Services
Gary Public Schools
Gary, Indiana*

Dr. Carlton W. H. Erickson (D)
*Director, Audio-Visual Center
University of Connecticut
Storrs, Connecticut*

Miss Ruth M. Ersted (A)
Supervisor of School Libraries

*State Department of Education
St. Paul, Minnesota*

Dr. Gene Faris (D)
*Associate Professor of Education
Audio-Visual Center
Indiana University
Bloomington, Indiana*

Dr. William R. Fulton (D)
*Professor of Education
The University of Oklahoma
Norman, Oklahoma*

Dr. Robert Gerletti (D)
*Director, Division of Educational
   Media
Los Angeles City Schools
Los Angeles, California*

Miss Mae Graham (A)
*Assistant Director
Division of Library Extension
State Department of Education
Baltimore, Maryland*

Dr. Frances Henne, Chairman (A)
*Professor, School of Library
   Service
Columbia University
New York, New York*

*(A) after the name of the Committee member indicates a representative of the American Association of School Librarians and (D) indicates a representative of the Department of Audiovisual Instruction of the National Education Association.

Miss Phyllis Hochstettler (A)
Associate Professor
School of Education
Portland State College
Portland, Oregon

Dr. Anna Hyer, Director (D)
Department of Audiovisual
*   Instruction*
National Education Association
Washington, D.C.

Miss Sarah Jones (A)
Chief Library Consultant
State Department of Education
Atlanta, Georgia

Miss Laura Dell Justin (A)
Assistant Executive Secretary
American Association of
*   School Librarians*
Washington, D.C.

Dr. Gaylen B. Kelley (D)
Associate Professor
School of Education
Boston University
Boston, Massachusetts

Dr. Marcus Konick (D)
Director, Division of Humanities
Lock Haven State College
Lock Haven, Pennsylvania

Dr. Wesley C. Meierhenry (D)
Assistant Dean
Teachers College
University of Nebraska
Lincoln, Nebraska

Mr. Barry Morris (D)
Assistant Superintendent for
*   Finance*
Fairfax County Schools
Fairfax, Virginia

Dr. Kenneth Norberg (D)
Professor of Education
Coordinator, Audiovisual Services

Sacramento State College
Sacramento, California

Miss Helen F. Rice (A)
Coordinator of Curriculum and
*   Instruction and School*
*   Libraries*
West Irondequoit School
*   District #3*
Rochester, New York

Mr. John Rowell (A)
Associate Professor
School of Library Science
Case Western Reserve University
Cleveland, Ohio

Mrs. Lillian L. Shapiro (A)
Librarian, Springfield Gardens
*   High School*
Springfield Gardens, New York

Dr. Mendel Sherman (D)
Assistant Director
Audio-Visual Center
Indiana University
Bloomington, Indiana

Mrs. Sara Srygley (A)
Professor, School of Library
*   Science*
Florida State University
Tallahassee, Florida

Mr. A. K. Trenholme (D)
Director, Department of
*   Instructional Materials*
Portland Public Schools
Portland, Oregon

Dr. John Vergis (D)
Professor of Education
Arizona State University
Tempe, Arizona

Miss Carolyn Whitenack (A)
Chairman, Department of
*   Educational Media*
Purdue University
West Lafayette, Indiana

iv

Members of the advisory board

American Association of School Administrators
Dr. William J. Ellena, Deputy Secretary, American Association of School Administrators.

American Institute of Architects
Mr. Paul M. Cope, Jr., Philadelphia, Pennsylvania.

American Personnel and Guidance Association
Mrs. Adelaide Siegel, Specialist for Professional Information, American Personnel and Guidance Association.

Association for Childhood Education International
Miss Clarissa Bacon, former Mary E. Leeper Fellow, Association for Childhood Education International.

Association for Educational Data Systems
Mr. Charles G. Beaudoin, Director of Data Processing, Montgomery Junior College, Rockville, Maryland.

Association for Supervision and Curriculum Development
Dr. Lauren Schwisow, Assistant Superintendent of Schools for Instruction, Hinsdale, Illinois.

Association of Chief State School Audio-visual Officers
Dr. Marcus Konick, Director, Division of Humanities, Lock Haven State College, Lock Haven, Pennsylvania.

Association of Classroom Teachers
Mrs. Dorothy R. Crawford, Librarian, Second Ward Senior High School, Charlotte, North Carolina.

Association of School Business Officials
Dr. Ridgley M. Bogg, Assistant Superintendent for Business Affairs, Great Neck Public Schools, Great Neck, New York.

Association of State School Library Supervisors
Miss Ruth M. Ersted, Supervisor of School Libraries, Minnesota State Department of Education, St. Paul, Minnesota.

The Catholic Library Association
The Reverend Father John R. Whitley, C.S.B., Aquinas Institute, Rochester, New York.

Council of Chief State School Officers
Miss Blanche Crippen, Assistant Executive Secretary, Council of Chief State School Officers.

Department of Elementary-Kindergarten-Nursery Education
(National Education Association)
Miss S. Adelaide Dale, Elementary Supervisor, Fairfax County Public Schools, Fairfax, Virginia.

Department of Elementary School Principals
(National Education Association)
Mr. Albert U. Kopf, Principal, Jefferson School, Maplewood, New Jersey.

Department of Foreign Languages
(National Education Association)
Miss Louise Winfield, Foreign Language Supervisor, Montgomery County Public Schools, Rockville, Maryland.

Department of Rural Education
(National Education Association)
Miss Evelyn R. Hodgdon, Formerly Professor of Education, New York State University, Oneonta, New York.

International Reading Association
Dr. Lillian Putnam, Professor of Education, Newark State College, Union, New Jersey.

National Association of Educational Broadcasters
Mr. George L. Hall, Research Associate, National Association of Educational Broadcasters.

National Association of Independent Schools
Mr. Lee Finks, Librarian, Episcopal High School, Alexandria, Virginia.

National Association of Secondary School Principals
Mr. L. Lee Lindley, Principal, Pikesville Senior High School, Baltimore, Maryland.
Mr. Murel G. Burdick, Principal, Muskegon Senior High School, Muskegon, Michigan.

National Catholic Education Association
Sister Mary Heffernan, Associate Secretary, National Catholic Education Association.

National Committee for the Support of Public Schools
Mrs. Alan Barth, Washington, D.C.

National Congress of Parents and Teachers
Miss Lucille Nix, Chairman, Reading and Library Service Committee, National Congress of Parents and Teachers.

National Council for the Social Studies
Dr. Helen McCracken Carpenter, Professor of History, Trenton State College, Trenton, New Jersey.

National Council of Teachers of English
Mrs. Frances Wimer, Head, Department of English, George Wythe High School, Richmond, Virginia.

National Council of Teachers of Mathematics
Mr. Lucien T. Hall, Jr., Mathematics Coordinator, Thomas Jefferson High School, Richmond, Virginia.

National Science Teachers Association
Dr. Marjorie H. Gardner, Associate Professor of Science Education, Departments of Chemistry and Secondary Education, University of Maryland, College Park, Maryland.

National Society for Programmed Instruction
Mrs. Gail L. Baker, Education and Training Analyst, Education and Training Division, Computer Applications Incorporated, Silver Spring, Maryland.

Preface

Purpose

The standards presented in this publication have been prepared by a Joint Committee of the American Association of School Librarians and the Department of Audiovisual Instruction of the National Education Association in cooperation with an Advisory Board consisting of representatives from twenty-eight professional and civic associations. Although the American Association of School Librarians revised their national standards in 1960[1] and the Department of Audiovisual Instruction released standards in 1966,[2] significant social changes, educational developments, and technological innovations have made it imperative to present new statements of standards. Adding impetus to the urgency for revision were the numerous requests from school administrators, audiovisual specialists, classroom teachers, curriculum specialists, school librarians, and other educators.

1. The American Association of School Librarians. *Standards for School Library Programs*. Chicago: American Library Association, 1960.

2. The Department of Audiovisual Instruction, National Education Association. *Quantitative Standards for Audiovisual Personnel, Equipment and Materials in Elementary, Secondary, and Higher Education,* developed by Gene Faris and Mendel Sherman. Washington, D.C.: Department of Audiovisual Instruction, National Education Association, January 1966. (Mimeographed)

Fulton, William R. *Criteria Relating to Educational Media Programs in School Systems.* Available from the Department of Audiovisual Instruction, National Education Association. (Mimeographed)

Both titles are parts of a study conducted under the auspices of the United States Office of Education, National Defense Education Act Program.

When the question of revising standards was first discussed, it became clear that standards for media programs would be greatly strengthened if they were prepared jointly by the two professional associations most closely identified with the resources for teaching and learning in the schools, and issued as a single document. Plans for cooperative action were initiated and successfully completed.

Two objectives that have motivated this project are: (1) to bring standards in line with the needs and requirements of today's educational goals and (2) to coordinate standards for school library and audiovisual programs.

The most important aim, of course, is to present standards for media programs that will best aid the schools in implementing their educational goals and instructional programs. The standards are designed for schools seeking to give young people education of good quality. Schools with innovative curricula and instructional techniques will need and want to go beyond the quantitative standards, but for schools which have not yet fully achieved their objectives, the standards can serve as a guide for charting goals to be reached in progressive steps over a planned period of time.

National standards have many functions beyond the immediate ones of providing guidelines for media programs of good quality and establishing criteria for the media services, resources, and facilities essential in the educational process. They act as a stimulus to correct the serious deficiencies now existing in too many of our schools by (1) assisting in the establishment of media centers where no service is available, or (2) accelerating the improvement of media services in those schools where optimum programs are defeated because of lack of sufficient staff and resources or because of other substandard conditions.

National standards for media programs are higher, quantitatively, than state and regional standards. The more important qualitative standards, representing the essential services to teachers and students, depend for their full implementation upon the conditions noted in these quantitative measures. Thus the standards lend support to the many schools which have achieved excellence in their educational programs and give assistance to those schools which are striving to attain this goal. Over the years, the national standards have tended to improve state standards, as can be witnessed in the recent endorsements by many states of the 1960 national school library standards and the 1966 audiovisual standards to serve as the standards for their states. Although there is often a time lag between the appearance of national standards and their achievement on a wide scale, the standards are not visionary but firmly based on the very real educational needs of today.

Because of the rapidity of change in educational, technological, and other fields, the Joint Committee recognizes that national standards require continuous revision, and recommends that such revisions be made at least biennially.

Terminology

Administrative and organizational patterns for materials and services vary among schools, as does the terminology used to describe them. There are school libraries, instructional materials centers, learning resource centers, library media centers, and others. In addition to that part of the school bearing one of these names, many schools also have a separate audiovisual department which, in turn, is designated in a variety of ways — communications center, audiovisual center, instructional media center, or other title. Confusion of terminology also exists with reference to the personnel, programs, and the centers or departments concerned with media at system, regional, and state levels.

In this publication, the term *media* refers to printed and audiovisual forms of communication and their accompanying technology. Other basic terms include *media program, media specialist,* and *media center. Media center* applies to the individual school. When reference is made to the next larger organizational unit, *system media center* is used. References to *school building* or *building level* mean an individual school, including those schools which have more than one building. These and other terms are defined on pages xv and xvi.

The terms *media program, media specialist,* and *media center* are used in this publication for purposes of convenience, consistency, and clarification within the context of the standards, and are not employed with an intent to mandate any particular title or terminology.

Scope

The standards presented in this publication describe the services of the media program in the school and note the requirements for the staff, resources, and facilities needed to implement the program effectively. Standards for personnel, resources, expenditures, and facilities are presented for a unified media program, but are applicable in schools having separate school libraries and audiovisual centers.

The standards apply to schools[3] having 250 or more students, but can also serve as valid guidelines for superior schools with fewer than 250 students that have or are planning a functional media program.

For schools which include Grades K-12 and for some special grade combinations (for example, schools with one grade only or schools that have two primary grades only), adaptations in the standards will have to be made. The basic philosophy of making materials in all media easily accessible and of providing the services of media specialists pertains to all schools.

Media programs in new school buildings are not treated separately, since new schools require media centers and programs comparable to those recommended for established schools. In order to have the media center in full operation when the new school opens, planning must be done in advance and sufficient time and funds must be provided for this purpose. The appointment of at least one full-time media specialist and clerk to work a year in advance of the opening of a new school is essential.

This document is directed to the media program in the individual school. References to system media centers are included whenever this information affects the interpretation of standards

3. The standards in this publication do not cover the specialized services and other needs of schools for handicapped children. Standards for students in schools for the deaf are presented in *Standards for Library-Media Centers in Schools for the Deaf—A Handbook for the Development of Library-Media Programs.* Washington, D.C.: Captioned Films for the Deaf, United States Office of Education, [1967]. Sponsored by The American Instructors of the Deaf.

for school buildings. The final chapter describes relationships between school media centers and media programs at the system level, and notes, very briefly, some characteristics of regional and state media services. The Joint Committee recommends that standards for media programs at these higher organizational levels and proposals for national planning be undertaken in the very near future.

The commentary accompanying the standards does not represent a complete description of the policies, services, activities, organization, administration, and operation of school media programs. It is not the purpose of this statement of standards to cover content available in textbooks and in other literature of the media field. It should be noted here that many principles contained in the statements of national standards referred to in the first paragraph of this preface are still pertinent.

Procedures

After a meeting of the Advisory Board and after the first two meetings of the Joint Committee, the tentative recommendations for the quantitative standards for media centers in individual schools and for the unified program were presented at special sessions during the 1967 conventions of the Department of Audiovisual Instruction, the American Association of School Librarians, and the National Education Association. Reactions were invited and received. These standards were also discussed in numerous other conferences and meetings. Several thousand individuals had an opportunity to express their viewpoints during this stage of the standards. A great number indicated their opinions and suggestions. These responses were reviewed and considered carefully by the members of the Joint Committee as they compiled the text of the standards.

The revised draft of the standards was then submitted to over two hundred specialists in the school library and audiovisual fields (including board members of the organizations sponsoring the project, presidents of state associations, and others). Additional comments from the field were studied by the members of the Joint Committee as they continued their work on the standards in later meetings. The members of the Advisory Board then met to review the draft approved by the Joint Committee, and after their recommendations had been incorporated, the standards were presented to the boards of the American Association of School Librarians and the Department of Audiovisual Instruction.

The Joint Committee, the Advisory Board, and the professional associations and civic organizations which they represent express their deepest gratitude for the assistance received through grants from the J. Morris Jones–World Book Encyclopedia – ALA Goals Award and from the U.S. Office of Education National Defense Education Act, Title VII, Part B Program, and to the many individuals throughout the nation who participated in, and contributed to, the shaping of the standards.

Definitions

Only selected definitions are included here. For common educational terms see *The Common Core of State Educational Information,* Washington, D.C.: U.S. Department of Health, Education, and Welfare, Office of Education, 1953, and subsequent volumes in the handbook series, *State Educational Records and Reports.*

Media — Printed and audiovisual forms of communication and their accompanying technology.

Media program — All the instructional and other services furnished to students and teachers by a media center and its staff.

Media center — A learning center in a school where a full range of print and audiovisual media, necessary equipment, and services from media specialists are accessible to students and teachers.

Media staff — The personnel who carry on the activities of a media center and its program.

Media specialist — An individual who has broad professional preparation in educational media. If he is responsible for instructional decisions, he meets requirements for teaching. Within this field there may be several types of specialization, such as (a) level of instruction, (b) areas of curriculum, (c) type of media, and (d) type of service. In addition other media specialists, who are not responsible for instructional decisions, are members of the professional media staff and need not have teacher certification, e.g., certain types of personnel in television and other media preparation areas.

Media technician — A media staff member who has training below the media specialist level, but who has special competencies in one or more of the following fields: graphics production and display, information and materials processing, photographic production, and equipment operation and simple maintenance.

Media aide — A media staff member with clerical or secretarial competencies.

System media center — A center at the school system level to provide supporting and supplemental services to school media centers in individual schools of the system.

Unified media program — A program in which instructional and other services related to both print and audiovisual media are administered in a single unified program under one director.

Teaching station — Any part of the school (usually but not always a classroom) where formal instruction takes place. Media centers are not included within this definition, although it is recognized that instruction is part of the media program.

Contents

The media program in the school

Media in the educational process

The process of education is essentially creative. It employs the intellectual, physical, and social skills of pupils in a learning process which begins with a clear enunciation of desirable human values as expressed in attitudes and actions of students. To secure these outcomes, the teacher and the media specialist must be aware of those characteristics which can guide most effectively the learner's development. The educational experiences which will be most helpful must be identified, and the most effective tools and materials located. The pupil will not only need to learn skills of reading, but those of observation, listening, and social interaction. He will need to develop a spirit of inquiry, self-motivation, self-discipline, and self-evaluation. He will need to master knowledge and to develop skills. Ultimately he must communicate his ideas with his fellows. In this entire process the media program, its staff, and its center play vital roles. Media convey information, affect the message, control what is learned, and establish the learning environment. They will help to determine what the pupil sees and what his attitude will be toward the world in which he lives. Therefore, it is important that every media specialist participate actively in shaping the learning environment and the design of instruction, and that every media facility, piece of equipment, book, or material be selected, produced, and used so that the students in our schools are challenged to a dynamic participation in a free, exciting, and enriched life.

The resources and services of the media center are a fundamental part of this educational process. One important aspect is that of enabling students and teachers to make a multimedia or intermedia approach to and use of materials in a unified media program. The availability of many materials in a variety of formats gives students and teachers the opportunity to select from among many resources the media best suited to answer their specific needs.

The philosophy of a unified program of audiovisual and printed services and resources in the individual school is one that has continuously grown and been strengthened in the last thirty years. This fusion of media resources and services provides optimum service for students and teachers. Many schools now have unified media programs. For those others that have separate audiovisual departments and school libraries, it is recommended that, wherever possible, these services be combined, administratively and organizationally, to form a unified media program. New schools should start with a unified media center and program of services.

The media program—a resource for learning

The student turns to and depends on the media program for many purposes—most of them related to curricular requirements but some initiated by other interests and needs. The media center's program, collections, and environment provide a broad spectrum of learning opportunities for large and small groups of students as well as for individual students. The focus of the media program is on facilitating and improving the learning process in its new directions—with emphasis on the learner, on ideas and concepts rather than on isolated facts, and on inquiry rather than on rote memorization.

Some media specialists have as their primary goal and responsibility the guidance of students in studying effectively, thinking objectively, and acquiring interest in and enthusiasm for exploration and research. Other media specialists work directly with the

2

teachers, helping them in clarifying objectives of student performance and in developing the means to reach these objectives and to evaluate the results. Additional media specialists are involved in various aspects of procuring, producing, storing, and retrieving media at the time and place needed for most effective learning.

Media are in the format most appropriate for the learning task. The emphasis is always upon the learner and upon the function of the media staff as a supportive arm to the teacher in achieving the goals of the instructional program.

The media program is indispensable in the educational programs that now stress individualization, inquiry, and independent learning for students. The extent to which current curricula emphasize self-directed learning is generally a matter of degree rather than of direction. In some schools, two-fifths or more of the student's time may be devoted to this form of learning. In programs that provide systematically, through modular and flexible scheduling or in other ways, for the time the student spends in individual exploration and independent learning, the media specialist, the classroom teacher or teachers involved, and the student form a team that plans and guides the student's work. Throughout, the media specialist remains in close contact with the teachers. The move away from textbook-dominated teaching and from teacher-dominated teaching has made the school media center a primary instructional center that supports, complements, and expands the work of the classroom.

The services and facilities of the media program give the student opportunities to create and produce materials. In some instances these activities have afforded the student his first experience of success and accomplishment.

The media program—a resource for teaching

The media specialist, who is knowledgeable about the learning process, childhood and adolescent growth, and curriculum development, works closely with teachers. Teachers find within the media program the resources, rich in depth and quantity and varied in format, that they require to meet the demands of innovative instructional methods. They look to the media specialist to

3

provide information about new materials; to make these materials easily and quickly accessible; to produce needed materials; to assist them in keeping informed about recent developments in their subject areas and in educational trends; to channel information to them regarding students' progress and problems; to organize and conduct inservice courses on the full spectrum of media and their uses; to instruct students in the use and resources of the media center as the needs of the curriculum indicate; and, increasingly, to assist in the analysis of instructional needs and the design of learning activities.

The most effective media program depends upon the support of the school principal and upon an ongoing partnership between teachers and media specialists. Teachers, as members of this team, keep media specialists informed about curricular content and assignments. Teachers are also involved in planning media instruction, evaluating resources, motivating the use of the media center, and implementing the media program.

The elements of the media program

A media program provides:

Consultant services to improve learning, instruction, and the use of media resources and facilities

Instruction to improve learning through the use of printed and audiovisual resources

Information on new educational developments

New materials created and produced to suit special needs of students and teachers

Materials for class instruction and individual investigation and exploration

Efficient working areas for students, faculty, and media staff

Equipment to convey materials to the student and teacher

The services, resources, and facilities represented in these separate but unified elements of the media program are described in more detail in the chapters that follow. Each part is dependent upon the other for the successful operation of the media program.

Basic to the success of a media program is the support that comes from school board members, school administrators, curriculum specialists, classroom teachers, and other citizens. The concern for education of high quality is shared by all—the educator, the community, and the government. As an important representative of the community, the school board member takes an active part in projecting and achieving goals for the school system. By his awareness of the educational needs of his community, he lends forceful support to financial programs which may be required in order to establish excellent schools supported by the necessary media programs, staff, resources, and facilities outlined in this publication. The school administrator, as a leader in the educational enterprise, is a strong influence in the encouragement of innovative curriculum design and teaching. In setting priorities for achieving educational objectives, he has the opportunity to press for the kind of fundamental support which a strong media program supplies to exemplary teaching and successful learning.

Education of high quality is expensive, but far more costly is the waste of human resources in poorly educated students whose talents are lost to this nation. Quality education requires media personnel in sufficient number and with specialized competencies. It calls for resources in great quantity and many forms. It needs facilities of adequate size and functional design. Today, educators and other citizens realize that educational programs of vitality, worth, and significance to students and to society depend upon excellent media services and resources in the schools.

2

Staff and services in the media program

Media specialists, assisted by technicians and aides, make unique and vital contributions to the total educational program of the school. Staff in sufficient number and with a variety of competencies is an indispensable part of a functional media center. Personnel qualified to implement the many diverse services are essential for the selection, organization, and effective use of a wide spectrum of educational media.

The first section of this chapter describes the services and responsibilities of the media specialists, standards for the size of the professional staff in the school, and recommendations concerning professional education and qualifications. The second section includes information about supportive staff members in the school's media program.

Professional staff

Services

The professional staff provides teachers and students with a wide variety of services. In so doing, the media specialists make instructional decisions within their purview and supply appropriate leadership in the educational process. The media specialist has status equal to that of other faculty members with comparable qualifications and responsibilities.

The professional staff implements the media program by:

Serving as instructional resource consultants and materials specialists to teachers and students

Selecting materials for the media center and its program

Making all materials easily accessible to students and teachers

Assisting teachers, students, and technicians to produce materials which supplement those available through other channels

Working with teachers in curriculum planning

Working with teachers to design instructional experiences

Teaching the effective use of media to members of the faculty

Assuming responsibility for providing instruction in the use of the media center and its resources that is correlated with the curriculum and that is educationally sound. Although most of this instruction will be done with individual students in the media center, some can be presented by teachers and media specialists in the center or in the classroom, with the size of the group to be instructed determined by teaching and learning needs.

Assisting children and young people to develop competency in listening, viewing, and reading skills

Helping students to develop good study habits, to acquire independence in learning, and to gain skill in the techniques of inquiry and critical evaluation

Guiding students to develop desirable reading, viewing, and listening patterns, attitudes, and appreciations

Providing teachers with pertinent information regarding students' progress, problems, and achievements, as observed in the media center

Acting as resource persons in the classrooms when requested by the teachers

Serving on teaching teams. The activities of the media specialist include acting as a resource consultant for teachers, designing media, and working directly with the students in their selection and evaluation of materials and in their research and other learning activities. Where the size of

8

the media staff permits, the media specialist would be a full-time member of the teaching team.

Making available to the faculty, through the resources of the professional collection, information about recent developments in curricular subject areas and in the general field of education

Supplying information to teachers on available inservice workshops and courses, professional meetings, and educational resources of the community

Various possibilities for allocation of staff responsibilities and services exist:

In elementary schools, the variations in pupil maturation and in learning patterns may make advantageous the allocation of media staff responsibilities by grade levels or age groups of students. In secondary schools, it will probably be more valuable to distribute staff responsibilities according to the subject areas of the curriculum.

During a transitional stage, when separate library and audiovisual departments are merging to form a unified center, it probably will be necessary to organize staff work according to type of media, i.e., print and audiovisual materials. If this is the case, the utmost care should be taken to see that students and teachers receive quick and effective service, without having to move constantly from the service area of one type of media to that of another.

Media specialists who concentrate most of their work in one area, whether by age, subject, or media, must still have competencies beyond these boundaries. Working with the users of the media program means dealing with a variety of students, a variety of needs, a variety of situations, and a variety of resources.

When a school has specialized media programs such as television, remote access, and language laboratories, the size of the media staff should be increased to include specialists in these areas. In a school which has a closed circuit television studio, for example, there will be need for at least a professional television producer and a television technician. The duties of the professional staff member include advising the teaching staff on

9

television production and writing, assisting with the preparation of scripts, designing visuals, and other educational and creative activities connected with this program.

If there is more than one media center or if there are resource or auxiliary centers, each of these areas must be staffed by one or more media specialists as well as by supportive personnel. Each center or branch thus has a media specialist in charge, who is responsible to and under the administrative authority of the head of the media program in the school.

Head of the media center

When there are two or more professional staff members, one is appointed as the head. This head of the media program in the school must have leadership, good public relations, and administrative ability. In addition, he should have competencies in both school library and audiovisual areas as well as knowledge in fields of learning theory, communications, and curriculum development.

In those schools having separate audiovisual and library programs but now implementing a unified program, the head of the media program may be either the former head of the audiovisual department or the former head of the school library. If one of these has competencies in both school library and audiovisual areas plus the qualities of administrative leadership, that individual should be named head. If neither has the combined background in school library and audiovisual fields, that media person who has superior qualifications of leadership, public relations, and administrative abilities and who has demonstrated the capability to serve both students and teachers should be appointed head of the program.

A unified media program is recommended in these standards. It is recognized that in some situations separate library and audiovisual programs will continue until such time as integration of the media program can be effected under the leadership of a qualified professional. In these instances, it is of utmost importance that the two programs be closely coordinated at the next higher level of administrative authority.

In establishing new media programs at the building level, the first professional should have the broad qualifications just described. The second media professional should have preparation in fields that complement those of the first. If the major preparation of the first professional is in the library field, the second should have a specialty in the audiovisual field, and vice versa.

The head of the school media program:

Reports to and plans with the principal (or equivalent chief school officer)

Maintains appropriate lines of communication with the system media director

Has responsibility, subject to administrative approval, for planning and implementing the media center's program of services to students and teachers, for the formulation of the media selection policy, and for the selection, organization, and administration of all materials and equipment in the school

Plans the activities of the media center staff

Plans the expenditure of funds allotted to the school media program and keeps records of these disbursements

Works cooperatively to further the program of media services:
By individual conferences with administration and faculty
As a member of curriculum committees
As a member of textbook committees
As chairman of the media center faculty committee
As chairman of the media center student committee
As chairman of the school committee for planning the program of teaching students how to use the media center and its resources effectively and how to develop appropriate study methods

Assists administrative authorities in the selection of personnel for the media center program

Provides for inservice education to teachers and media center staff in the use of media and in the selection and utilization of materials

Creates, through knowledge of and skill in personnel administration, a professional atmosphere in which media staff members work harmoniously and at optimum level, and

in which students and teachers can take full advantage of
the resources and services of the media center

Has the status and position equivalent at least to that of chairman or head of a subject department in the school building,
and serves on the faculty council

Size of the professional staff

It is recommended that the media center have one full-time
media specialist for every 250 students, or major fraction thereof.
With professional staff in this number, the media program is
carefully planned and fully implemented, the resources of teaching and learning are wisely selected and made easily accessible,
and, most important, individualized media services to students
and teachers are provided in optimum measure.

Professional education and preparation

Regardless of the organizational arrangement for the media
program in which they work, all media specialists who are responsible for instructional decisions should acquire, as part of
their professional preparation, a knowledge of certain funda-
mentals in the general field of education and in areas related to
media resources and services. The former should contain content
dealing with curriculum structure, student growth and development, instructional methods, and psychology. The subject matter
in the media area should include: analysis, evaluation, selection,
and design of printed and audiovisual materials; procedures for
the utilization of materials by students, teachers, and other school
personnel; the objectives, functions, and program of the media
center; the administration and organization of materials and
media services; communications theory; and information science,
including the understanding of the theory and design of instructional systems. In both the general field and in the media area, the
content can be related to a specific school level (elementary,
secondary, or other).

In view of the rapid expansion and continuing change in
knowledge, communications, curricular developments, and technology, the need for specialization in the school media field and
in the professional education of media specialists has become

urgent. The professional education of media specialists must prepare them for the kinds of specialization that have been noted in the section dealing with the services of professional staff members.

This specialization can focus on level of school, subject matter, or type of media. Level of school specialization (usually elementary, middle, junior high, or high school) provides for media specialists informed in depth about the curriculum, instructional methods, media programs, and characteristics of students in schools of different grade levels. Subject matter specialization provides for media specialists knowledgeable about the discipline, its curricular developments, and its audiovisual and printed resources. Media specialization provides for specialists who understand the nature, creation, and instructional uses of specific media: television programs, electronic and computerized processes, programed instruction, and remote access systems.

These recommendations for specialization are not necessarily retroactive for staff now working in schools where the media center is in a transitional stage. The head of the media program and professional staff members could have a specialization in either print or audiovisual materials and services. It is strongly recommended, however, that inservice programs be provided and that all media specialists be encouraged to take advantage of the many avenues of continuing education (workshops, institutes, courses, and others) to update and expand their professional knowledge and competencies.

The qualifications and the professional education requirements for the staff of the system or state media program reflect the patterns of specialization already described. Where these centers exist, the kinds of special competencies represented on the staff can affect the range of specialization in the individual school.

All professionals who have responsibilities for making instructional decisions should be certified as qualified teachers.

Because of the many ongoing changes in media programs, the whole matter of professional education requires careful review. Not only do specifics of content need to be delineated but other problems merit study: the place, scope, and nature of undergraduate professional education; the types and programs of specialization; the relationships or sequences of undergraduate, fifth year, sixth year, and doctoral programs; and the criteria for accrediting or approving programs of professional education for media specialists in colleges and universities. In those universities and colleges having separate programs in library science and audiovisual instruction, the development of a unified or closely coordinated program is desirable. If only one program is presented, it is essential that its scope be broadened to cover resources and services relating to both print and audiovisual materials.

Certification

Certification, like professional education, needs study and evaluation. In many states, reviews of certification requirements affecting media specialists are now in process. These reviews are concerned with: requirements for various levels and positions in media centers; the kind and amount of professional education needed by media specialists; provisions and requirements for specialization within the field; and criteria for approving agencies of higher education which offer programs for the preparation of media specialists. Many of the problems requiring solution in the area of professional education have relevance for the study and evaluation of certification procedures.

Study and redefinition of certification requirements need to be undertaken in the light of currently accepted objectives of media centers, of services performed by media specialists, of recommended standards for size of staff, and of types of positions in centers having more than one media specialist. The principle has long been recognized that in centers having three or more professional staff members, some classification and gradation of professional education requirements are in order.

Certification requirements should neither hinder the development of excellent media programs in schools nor regiment the creativity and experimentation of the professional schools or departments.

As in the matter of professional education, the problems must be resolved concerning the dichotomy of certification — one for

14

school librarians and one for audiovisual specialists. Some kind of certification allowing for all the variant patterns that have been recognized seems essential. This not only would speed the development of unified media centers but would also help to correct the serious manpower problem and promote recruitment.

Supportive staff of the media center

The supportive staff of the media center in the school includes media technicians and media aides, who always work under the direction of a professional media specialist. These staff members have specific skills and special abilities that are necessary for a successful media program, and they make it possible for the media specialists to concentrate their time on professional services and activities. An inadequate number of supportive staff members results in a costly expenditure of professional time and talent in clerical, housekeeping, and technical tasks.

Services of media technicians

The size of the school and the organization of the media program and its staff at the system level may affect the number and kind of technicians needed at the building level. Good service to students and teachers is the determining criterion. This service at the building level includes, as a minimum, production of materials, repair and maintenance of equipment, and assistance with various kinds of media presentations and information processing. Technicians provide assistance in one or a combination of the following areas:

Graphics production and display. The technician assists media specialists and teachers by performing such tasks as: producing transparencies; making posters, charts, graphs, dioramas, and similar materials; arranging displays, exhibits, and bulletin boards; lettering; making slides; designing and illustrating promotion items and publications of the center; preparing materials for use with educational television; and other services.

Information and materials processing. The technician performs such tasks as: bibliographic searching, details of technical processing, assistance to teachers and students in locating materials, working at circulation desks, and other services.

Photographic production. The technician performs such tasks as: developing pictures for publicity, promotion, records, and other purposes; doing camera work involved in making films and producing television programs; photographing items for slides, filmstrips, and resource files; supervising the dark room; and other services.

Equipment operation and simple maintenance. The technician performs such tasks as: keeping in working order equipment for films, television, remote access, recordings, radio programs, and programed instruction; engineering these facilities, as required; handling the mechanics of computerized processes; and other services.

Services of media aides

Media aides do clerical and secretarial work such as typing, keeping records, sending notices, opening mail, and handling office and circulation routines. They are responsible for reading shelves, shelving and filing materials, inspection and repair of films, mounting pictures, and keeping the appearance of the center in good order.

It is assumed that the media aide is employed and paid by the school board. The volunteer service rendered by parents can have value, but it is not a substitute for trained and salaried workers. Provision should be made for a sufficient number of paid staff members to handle all secretarial, clerical, and maintenance work.

Unpaid student media assistants (both student library assistants and audiovisual assistants) are not the equivalent of media aides. If schools feel it advisable to provide students with a volunteer service program in the media center, such activities should receive service and not academic credit, and should not interfere with the academic program of students.

Size of supportive staff

In order to meet the needs of an effective media program and its diversified activities, it is recommended that at least one media technician and one media aide be employed for each professional media specialist in schools of 2000 or fewer students. As many additional aides and technicians should be appointed as are needed to support special media programs in the school, such as television broadcasting, remote access, and language laboratories. It is important that there be a technician with graphics ability in each school.

When the enrollment of the school exceeds 2000 students, the number of media aides and technicians might need to be adjusted. For that portion of the enrollment exceeding 2000, the ratio of supportive staff members to media specialists might be less than 2 to 1.

Selection, accessibility, and organization of materials

Meeting standards for the selection of materials and making the resources of teaching and learning easily accessible are necessary for (1) the provision of materials of good quality in the school, (2) optimum use of these materials by teachers, students, and the staff of the media center, and (3) the functional and efficient organization of materials.

This chapter includes three sections: general guidelines for the selection of materials, the accessibility of materials in the media center and in other areas of the school, and the organization of materials. Principles dealing specifically with the selection and organization of professional materials for teachers are presented in Chapter 4.

General guidelines for the selection of materials

The availability of federal and state funds, the avalanche of materials in all formats and different degrees of quality which are appearing on the market, and the increased pressures of commercialism in the sale of media have made the careful selection of materials critically important. The purchase of materials poor in quality or inappropriate for the needs of the school is a disservice to students and teachers, and is a wasteful expenditure of funds. The media specialists uphold standards that make certain that only acceptable materials of sufficient range and variety are acquired to meet the needs of the students and faculty in the school.

Policies

Basic policies that shape the selection of materials for the media center include:

1. The school and school system have a written statement of selection policy, formulated and endorsed by the school administration, the media specialists, and faculty, and adopted by the school board. This statement indicates the general objectives and procedures of selection, and affirms such American freedoms as described in the *Library Bill of Rights,*[1] the *School Library Bill of Rights,*[2] and *The Students' Right to Read.*[3]

2. The collection meets the requirements of the various curricular areas and provides for the diverse learning skills of individuals representing all levels and types of ability. Materials are also included that inspire and meet the independent interests and research needs of students. Therefore, the media collection is rich in breadth and depth in the subjects covered, the types of material included, and the forms of expression represented.

---

1. The *Library Bill of Rights* was adopted by the Council of the American Library Association in 1948 and revised in 1967.

2. The *School Library Bill of Rights* was approved by the American Association of School Librarians and endorsed by the Council of the American Library Association in 1955.

3. National Council of Teachers of English. *The Students' Right to Read.* Champaign, Ill.: the Council, 1962.

3. Media selection, distribution, and use reflect current trends in education and communications. Such developments as the multimedia approach to materials, the widespread use of paperbacks, and the emergence of information systems, instructional design, and computerized programs of learning and instruction have had a marked influence on the scope and use of materials in the school and in the media center. The findings of research in learning development, the increased sophistication of youth, the rising expectations of deprived young people, the crisis of the central city, and curricular innovations influence the selection of materials.

4. The selection of materials by a process of competent evaluation is the responsibility of qualified specialists at the local, state, regional, or national levels. The process of selection is expedited by consulting reviews, recommended lists, standard bibliographic tools, and special releases.

5. Sufficient duplicate copies of materials are available to meet the needs of students and teachers (discussed under the heading *Accessibility*). This is not identical with the provision of copying services. The latter necessitates adherence to the copyright law on the part of school administrators and media specialists in reproducing and making facsimile copies of copyrighted materials, both print and nonprint.

Procedures

The following principles refer to the selection and evaluation of materials, in all formats, which are acquired for the media program:

1. Media specialists in individual schools obtain the evaluations of qualified materials specialists outside the school building.

2. The cooperation of teachers and curriculum personnel in the selection of materials for the media center is always enlisted, and their suggestions receive priority consideration. In view of the heavy schedules of teachers and the vast quantities of materials on the market, teachers and curriculum personnel welcome, and must have, the services of qualified media specialists in selecting resources for teaching and learning in the school. This partnership between media specialists and other members of

21

the faculty indicates the desirability of including the study of media resources within the professional education of teachers and administrators.

3. Materials are planned and created within the media center by teachers, students, media specialists, and technicians when commercially available materials are not suitable or need supplementation. Locally produced resources not only supplement these materials, but they also provide learning opportunities for the students who create them.

4. Final responsibility for the selection of materials is vested in the principals and head media specialists in the schools.

5. Evaluation of materials in the media collections is a continuous process. Media specialists in the schools constantly reevaluate materials after they are acquired. Suitability for the users of the media center is a major criterion, but such established elements of evaluation as accuracy, values, up-to-dateness, and style are also considered.

Accessibility of materials

In the media center

Optimum use of materials is facilitated in many ways:

1. Resources of the media center and services of professional staff members are available whenever needed by students and teachers. The formal and informal instructional program of the media center — whether for individuals, classes, small groups, teaching teams, or other combinations of students and teachers — requires a qualified staff of sufficient number to achieve its objectives. If the number and qualifications of staff personnel are substandard, the resources of the center, no matter how extensive, cannot be used to their fullest potential.

2. The media center is open at all times of the school day, and also before and after school. In order to expand services to students and teachers and to obtain greater returns from the school's investment in materials and equipment, these hours are being extended to include evenings, Saturdays, and vacation periods. This extended program is, however, dependent upon certain conditions. The geographic location of the school must be one

that students can reach safely and easily. The location of the media center in the school should make it possible to keep the center open within reasonable limits of maintenance costs and with adequate security measures after regular school hours. Plans for new schools should therefore show a location for the media center on a ground floor with an outside entrance and with provisions for remaining open when the rest of the school plant is closed. Some cooperative arrangements may be made among a group of schools to rotate evening hours of service so that one media center at a time is open to students.

Whatever arrangement is followed, the extended hours of service require additional professional and supportive staff, preferably working on a staggered schedule rather than as a separate staff. The total work time for a professional staff member should be equivalent to the average work load and schedule of other faculty members.

The media center should not be used for functions which interfere with its use by students.

3. Recent inventions such as audio and video remote access and projected materials through television sets provide new channels for making resources accessible in the media center, throughout the school, and in the home.

4. Full accessibility entails not only the availability of a collection of materials that meets standards for variety, breadth, and scope, but also the provision of duplicate copies of titles to meet curricular requirements as well as requests of students for popular materials that are not necessarily related to class work. The use of paperbacks is valuable in meeting heavy demands of students and for encouraging pleasure in reading. Duplicate copies of filmstrips, 8mm films, recordings, and other materials are provided to meet the needs of students and teachers.

5. Media equipment in sufficient amounts must be available to assure maximum accessibility and use of materials by groups and individuals. Generous acquisition of microfilm, films, filmstrips, and recordings is paradoxically negated if the equipment needed for their use is provided in too limited number. Lack of such tools hinders individualization of learning and effective teaching.

6. The design, facilities, and arrangement of the media center are planned for the convenience and comfort of the users (see Chapter 5 for details about space and equipment).

7. Circulation and loan regulations permit students and teachers to obtain materials easily for use throughout the school and at home. Only in very exceptional cases should materials be barred from loan outside the media center. Duplicate copies of reference works are available for borrowing, as are all types of print and nonprint materials. Students borrow whatever materials they need, and technological advances make it practical for them to borrow the equipment as it becomes more portable. Loan regulations are generous and elastic, with lengths of loan easily renewable unless there is reasonable justification for limitations. The quantity of material that can be withdrawn at any one time is not limited.

8. Accessibility involves the utilization of the resources and services of the system or regional media center (see Chapter 6). These may include inter-center loan materials, televised and taped programs originating in the district center, resources in banks of materials, and films and other materials channeled into the classrooms and media center areas. These expanded services increase considerably the accessibility of resources to students and teachers and contribute further to the variety, richness, and efficiency of the media program in the school.

9. Individuals or small groups of children in elementary schools have access to the media center at all times during the school day. The use of a rigid schedule for class visits to the center is not recommended.

In the classrooms and other teaching areas

Resources of the center are made easily accessible throughout the school. Materials from the media center are sent to classrooms and other teaching areas not served directly by a formally organized branch of the media center on a long or short term loan basis. The media center staff assists teachers and students in the selection and use of appropriate materials for these classroom collections. The same need for providing sufficient copies of audiovisual materials exists as for books. The use of such sources as filmstrips and 8mm films is important, and each student should have access to materials and necessary equipment in the classroom and other teaching areas.

Basic information tools — encyclopedias, dictionaries, globes, and similar materials — are available in the classrooms for indefinite loan periods, but remain the responsibility of the center for selection, upkeep, and replacement. The provision of supplementary resources, such as sets of textbooks, magazines, newspapers, and audiovisual materials, is arranged through the media center whenever they are needed in the classroom or other teaching areas.

Methods of administering textbooks which students are required to have vary among schools, but there is widespread agreement that these books fall within the organizational framework of the media center and should be administered by the head of the media program. Media specialists are included in the committees responsible for the selection of textbook materials. It must be emphasized, however, that if responsibility for the acquisition, organization, distribution, collection, and maintenance of textbooks is delegated to the media center, additional staff, space, and funds must be provided beyond those recommended elsewhere in this publication. Most of the work should be performed by clerical workers and not by media specialists whose functions, in these situations, are supervisory in nature.

Paperbacks are frequently used as required textbooks and as such, should be provided by the school. Other paperbacks in large quantities are part of the media center's regular collection. If teachers wish to have a collection of paperbacks accessible in the classroom, these are made available from the media center's collection as part of the regular program by which the center provides teachers with all kinds of materials. The question of whether media centers should sell paperback books cannot be answered by any hard and fast regulations except to state that handling sales routines should not involve professional staff. The selection of paperbacks for sale in the center, the school bookstore, or elsewhere in the school does involve the professional competencies of the media specialists.

Organization of materials

It is imperative that materials be organized and arranged so that users of the center can obtain materials of all kinds quickly and easily.

The arrangement of materials in the media center follows some approved classification scheme. Rigid adherence to the numerical sequence of a classification scheme is not necessary if other groupings of resources make the materials more easily used, more accessible, or more inviting for exploration. A multimedia arrangement with printed and audiovisual resources on similar subjects shelved together is proving successful in some schools.

It is advisable to have materials cataloged and processed through some agency outside the school building. This insures skilled service, avoids duplication of effort, and provides maximum time for the professional staff of the school media center to work directly with students and teachers. Moreover, it makes materials immediately accessible upon their delivery to the school media center.

Arrangements for centralized processing are practical and recommended for any school system or cluster of cooperating schools. For many schools, centralized processing at the system level provides the most efficient and economical service. Regional centers, involving several school systems in some form of cooperative arrangement, are providing this service in some localities. Centralized processing on a statewide basis is being done in at least two states and is being studied in others.

Commercial processing is generally useful, especially for schools not having access to a system processing center. Services from these companies range from supplying catalog cards to the complete processing and cataloging of materials.

Changes and experimentation in the processing of materials will probably alter procedures in the near future. Computers, widely used for the purchase, accounting, invoicing, and acquisition of materials, give promise for radically changing catalogs of materials in the centers. The printed book catalog, still experimental, promises advantages and needs further study.

Another possibility is the cataloging of materials at the source, by the publisher or producer, in accordance with standards established by professional organizations.

4

The resources
of the media center:
size and
expenditures

The quantitative standards recommended for the materials collection are derived from the policies, procedures, and guidelines dealing with the selection, evaluation, and accessibility of resources described in Chapter 3. All materials must meet qualitative standards for selection and must be easily accessible. Provision must be made for sufficient duplication of titles of books, filmstrips, recordings, and other materials to meet curricular needs and other requests.

This chapter consists of three parts: the basic collections of the media center, professional materials for the faculty, and expenditures.

The basic collections of the media center

The standards recommended for the basic collections of the media center exclude the following resources: professional materials for the faculty (see pages 33-35); dictionaries, encyclopedias, magazines, and newspapers that are acquired for classroom use; and textbook collections.

The standards recommended for schools of 250 students or over are as follows:

Books	At least 6000-10,000 titles representing 10,000 volumes or 20 volumes per student, whichever is greater
Magazines	
Elementary school (K-6)	40-50 titles (includes some adult non-professional periodicals)
Elementary school (K-8)	50-75 titles
Junior high school	100-125 titles
Secondary school	125-175 titles
All schools	In addition: necessary magazine indexes and duplication of titles and indexes as required
Newspapers	
Elementary school	3-6 titles
Junior high school	6-10 titles
Secondary school	6-10 titles
All schools	One local, one state, and one national newspaper to be represented in the collection
Pamphlets, clippings, and miscellaneous materials	Pamphlets, government documents, catalogs of colleges and technical schools, vocational information, clippings, and other materials appropriate to the curriculum and for other interests of students
Filmstrips	500-1000 titles, representing 1500 prints or 3 prints per pupil, whichever is greater (the number of titles to be increased in larger collections)

8mm films
Single concept
Regular length[1]

1½ films per student with at least 500 titles supplemented by duplicates

16mm films

Acquisition of 16mm films at the building level would depend upon extent and frequency of use of individual film titles in the school, upon the availability of a system media center and its collection of film resources, and upon other factors.[2] Whatever the source, the films must be quickly and easily accessible to the students and teachers requiring them. The recommendation given below is stated in terms of accessibility. Recommended: access to a minimum of 3000 titles supplemented by duplicates and rentals

Tape and disc recordings
(excluding electronic laboratory materials)

1000-2000 titles representing 3000 records or tapes or 6 per student, whichever is greater (the number of titles to be increased in larger collections)

1. Because of the nature of certain media forms and the evolving or transitional development of others, quantitative recommendations cannot be given. Nevertheless, these materials make a unique contribution to the instructional program and provide resources for the academic needs and general interests of students. An abundant number should be available in the media center.
2. Absence of a quantitative recommendation should not be interpreted as meaning that it is not desirable for the media center in the individual school to have 16mm films in its collection. Former standards have indicated that a school should purchase films used six or more times a year, and that an annual rental fee for a film totaling from one-fifth to one-seventh of its purchase price generally indicates the feasibility of permanent acquisition. In at least one large metropolitan school system, experience indicated the value of a basic elementary school building collection of 300-400 film titles, with access to a central collection on a daily delivery basis.

| **Slides** | 2000 (including all sizes of slides) |

Graphic materials

Art prints (reproductions)	1000 with duplicates as needed
Pictures and study prints	Individual study prints and pictures for the picture and vertical file collections; in addition to individual prints, access to 15 sets per teaching station plus 25 sets available from the media center
Other graphics[1]	Posters, photographs, charts, diagrams, graphs, and other types

Globes

Elementary school	1 globe in each teaching station and 2 in the media center
Secondary school	1 globe per 5 teaching stations and 2 in the media center
All schools	In addition, special globes to be available in the media center
Maps	1 map for each region studied and special maps (economic, weather, political, historical, and others) for each area studied
	Duplicate maps available for each class section requiring maps at the same time, the number of duplicates to be determined by sections of students and the availability of maps on transparencies and filmstrips
	Wall maps for teaching stations

| **Microform** | To be purchased as available on topics in the curriculum. All periodical subscriptions indexed in *Reader's Guide* and newspaper files should be obtained as needed for reference. |

1. See footnote 1 on page 31.

Transparencies	2000 transparencies, plus a selection of subject matter masters

Other materials[1]

Programed instructional materials	Printed, electronic, and other forms of programed materials
Realia	Models, dioramas, replicas, and other types of realia

Kits
Art objects
Video tape recordings
Remote access programs
Resource files

Professional materials for the faculty

Administrators, classroom teachers, media specialists, and other members of the faculty must have easy access to professional materials for quick consultation and reference. These materials are necessary so that the staff can keep abreast of trends, developments, techniques, research and experimentation both in general and specialized educational fields. The professional collection can also be used by parents of students in the school.

The collection of professional materials in a system media center does not remove the need for a professional collection in the school building. Professional materials in the larger center are essentially supplementary in nature and are described in Chapter 6.

Recommended for the professional collection of books and periodicals in schools of 250 students or over are:

Books	200-1000 titles

Magazines	40-50 professional titles, with duplicates as needed; also *Education Index*

1. See footnote 1 on page 31.

The professional collection also includes the following types of materials: courses of study, curriculum guides, teacher's manuals, government documents, films and filmstrips, tapes, pamphlets, education materials released by the state and community, catalogs of materials such as paperbacks and films, catalogs and brochures of museums and sites of educational value, television and radio program guides and manuals, field trip evaluations, indexes of community resources, releases of teachers' organizations and associations, announcements of professional meetings, and releases on workshops, courses, and other programs for continuing education.

In addition to the usual areas of general and specialized education represented, it is desirable to have works in such related subjects as communications, sociology, anthropology, behavioral psychology, linguistics, philosophy, and others. Paperback books are readily and inexpensively available in many of these areas, making it economically possible for every school to have a valuable and stimulating collection for the teaching staff. Some of these titles, useful to secondary school students in their research, are duplicated in the collection of the media center.

The head of the media center, as the official administrator of the professional collection, follows the same principles for service in this aspect of the media program as elsewhere:

1. Only worthwhile materials are obtained, with teachers being involved in their selection.
2. Materials are made easily accessible and are circulated to teachers for use in the classroom or at home.
3. Duplicate copies are purchased as the demand requires.
4. The collection is kept up-to-date.
5. Materials are borrowed from the system or regional center to meet specific requests of teachers or to bring an assortment of materials to the attention of the faculty.

The media center staff keeps teachers informed of materials added to the collection and brings to their attention specific items, print and non-print, that will be of particular interest or value. The services of the media center include making, upon request, facsimile reproductions of materials not subject to copyright restrictions.

The professional collection is housed in a convenient location, affording privacy for the teachers. The surroundings are attractive and comfortable. This area is equipped for use of audiovisual materials.

The organization of the school's instructional program or architectural plan may require several resource centers for teachers in an individual school. In some existing situations, separate resource centers are provided by the media center for teaching teams, for departments, or for teachers in schools within a school. These collections are located in the areas allocated for these special aspects of the instructional program, and are centrally cataloged.

Expenditures

To maintain an up-to-date collection of materials in the media center not less than 6 per cent of the national average for per pupil operational cost (based on average daily attendance) should be spent per year per student.[3] (The 1968-1969 estimated national average for per pupil expenditure is $680.00.[4]) These funds are used to purchase materials for both the individual school and the system media center.

As a result of recommendations from school administrators and school business managers, the amount for annual expenditures for materials in the media center is expressed in a single figure. Flexibility is desirable in order to achieve balanced collections and to meet the quantitative standards for the varied materials. Ordinarily, half of the annual appropriation should be spent on printed materials and half on audiovisual materials.

The amount recommended for the annual expenditure for resources provides for the acquisition of newly published or

3. Total operational cost, as described in school accounting procedures released by the United States Office of Education, includes administration, instruction, attendance services, health services, pupil transportation services, operation of plant, maintenance of plant, and fixed charges. (Paul L. Reason, Alpheus L. White, and others. *Financial Accounting for Local and State Systems: Standard Receipt and Expenditure Accounts.* Washington, D.C.: United States Office of Education, 1957, reprinted in 1965.)

4. National Education Association. Research Division. *Estimates of School Statistics, 1968-1969. (Research Report 1968-R16.)* Washington, D.C.: National Education Association, 1968. p. 20.

produced materials of value to the media program, needed materials other than those currently released, replacements of titles, and duplicates. This figure does not include funds for school-adopted textbooks, reference materials housed permanently in classrooms, closed circuit television installations, subscription television, electronic learning centers, distribution systems, supplies, equipment, and the processing of materials.

Funds for the initial collections of all materials in newly established media centers should come from capital outlay and not from the amount recommended for annual expenditures for materials. In those schools where the collections of the media centers do not meet standards for size and quality, additional funds will be required to augment the annual budget, while the schools are building their resources toward the standards recommended for materials of all kinds.

Recommendations for expenditures take into consideration the materials needed to implement the programs of schools which stress learning through independent study and inquiry and which place a high premium on individualization in the educational process. Special programs and curricular experimentation may require an upward revision of the amount suggested.

In providing annual funds for materials, it is important that no schools fall below 6 per cent per student per year of the current national average for per pupil operational costs. Schools spending less than this amount for operational costs would still need to appropriate funds for resources on the basis of the national average in order to have sufficient resources for teaching and learning. Many schools spending more than the national average for per pupil operational cost will want to use their own per pupil expenditure figure as the base for the 6 per cent appropriation for resources; in this manner a high quality media program can be developed and maintained to support a superior instructional program.

When there are two system media supervisors, one for audio-visual programs and one for school libraries, each should have administrative responsibility for the expenditure of funds appropriate in amount for the resources in his area (ordinarily not less than 3 per cent of the per pupil cost as described above).

When there is no system supervisor or system head of the media program, funds should be allocated to each building media program at the recommended rate of 6 per cent of the national per pupil cost. In all cases, there should be flexibility of purchasing procedures so that materials can be ordered throughout the year.

5

Media center facilities

The standards recommended for the facilities of the media center are designed to accommodate the resources and services of the media program that have been described. This chapter deals with the environment, location and space, and equipment of the center.

Environment

The media center is functional in design and inviting in appearance. It should have good lighting, acoustical treatment, and temperature and humidity control necessary for the comfort of its users and for the preservation of materials. Floor covering is made of noise-reducing materials. Carpeting is recommended.

Location and space

The center is located away from noise areas and in a place easily accessible to students and teachers. The location permits use of the center before and after school hours, evenings, Saturdays, and vacations. Extended hours of service are more easily administered when the media center is accessible without opening the entire school.

Variations exist among schools in the design and arrangement of media centers. In many elementary and secondary schools a single media center will effectively serve the needs of students and teachers. In large schools or in schools with innovative programs additional spaces may be needed. The recommendations for space that follow may therefore have to be expanded or adapted to meet the needs of the instructional program of a particular school, or to fit functionally into such architectural plans as schools within schools.

In addition to the single media center, there may be resource centers structured according to subject, grade level, or other school organizational patterns. For large schools, additional space may be provided by subdividing a large media center into smaller areas, such as separate subject rooms. In schools where the standard for the percentage of student enrollment exceeds a seating capacity of 100, a single center is undesirable unless the space is subdivided to create several areas within the center.

Whether there is one media center or several, the program is administered by the head media specialist. Resource centers or branches or divisions of the media center are staffed by professional and supportive staff, and adequate space is provided for the media resources and services.

The specifications that follow for space are based on an enrollment of 1000 students or fewer, and will need to be increased proportionately in larger schools. As already noted, additional space will usually be required when the media program has more than a single media center or a media center with resource or satellite centers.

The recommendations for space for the media program are as follows:

Functions	Special aspects	Space in square feet
Entrance Circulation and distribution	Displays and exhibits, copying equipment, card catalogs, periodical indexes	800-1000
Reading and browsing Individual viewing and listening	No more than 100 students should be seated in one area	Space based on 15 per cent of student enrollment at 40 sq. ft. per student[1]

1. Schools with fewer than 350 students should provide space for no less than 50 students.

Functions	Special aspects	Space in square feet
Individual study and learning Storytelling (elementary schools) Information services	30-40 per cent of seating capacity for individual study areas, equipped with power and capability of electronic and response systems and television outlets; area should be ducted for power and coaxial distribution Where carrels are used, suggested size is 36 in. wide and 24 in. deep, equipped with shelving and media facilities, including electrical power, television and response outlets Linear and other types of shelving for all types of materials	The instructional program in some schools may require that $\frac{1}{3}$ to $\frac{3}{4}$ of the student population be accommodated in the media center(s)
Conference rooms	Movable walls to allow for combining areas Electrical and television outlets and acoustical treatment One room, acoustically treated, with typewriters for student use	3-6 rooms with 150 sq. ft. each
Small group viewing and listening	In addition to space provided for conference rooms Electrical and television inputs and outlets, permanent wall screen, and acoustical treatment	200

Functions	Special aspects	Space in square feet
Group projects and instruction in research	Flexible space, the equivalent of a classroom area, equipped for instructional purposes and needs	900-1000
Administration	Office space for 4 professional staff members Media program planning area	600-800
Workroom	The amount of space recommended will have to be increased if centralized cataloging and processing services are not available from a system media center	300-400
Maintenance and repair service	Major service to come from system center	120-200
Media production laboratory	Sinks, running water, electrical outlets	800-1000
Dark room	Light-proof and equipped with light locks	150-200
Materials and equipment storage for production	Necessary temperature and humidity control	120
Stacks	Stacks for overflow books and audiovisual materials	400-800
Magazine storage	Space for back issues of magazines, readily accessible for use	250-400

Functions	Special aspects	Space in square feet
Audiovisual equipment: distribution and storage	Decentralized storage in large schools	400-600
Center for professional materials for faculty	Designed as a teachers' conference room Adjacent to media production laboratory	600-800

Optional space (determined by school program)

Television		
Studio	A soundproof studio with ceilings 15 ft. high and doors 14 ft. by 12 ft.	40 ft. by 40 ft. studio with necessary control space
Storage	For television properties, visuals, etc.	800-1000
Office with work space	Place back-to-back with television studio	1200
Radio	May be near television facilities	20 ft. by 25 ft. studio with necessary control space
Computerized learning laboratory	Facilities to have response capability	900-1000
Storage and control center for remote access		900-1000

Equipment

Specifications are readily available from many sources for shelving, tables, and chairs. Measurements in height and width recognize the physical differences of children at the elementary and secondary school levels. Shelving is adjustable and sufficient in linear feet to provide for the housing of the number and kinds of materials (see Chapter 4) and for expansion. Wall shelving allows maximum use of floor space, but some grouping of shelving sections can contribute to the accessibility of materials, the flexibility of arrangement within the room, and the creation of small inviting areas.

Special shelving and cabinets must be provided for such materials as picture books, records, audio and video tapes, filmstrips, films, magazines, microfilms, transparencies, maps, graphs, and pictures. In some schools nonprint materials are interfiled with the print materials, an arrangement that affects the type of shelving or storage selected.

The media center must have a sufficient number of electrical outlets, the necessary electrical power for peak loads, at least one telephone outlet, and intercommunication outlets. Light switches, electrical outlets, power grids, thermostats, telephones, and fire extinguishers should be conveniently located without using space needed for shelving.

It is unnecessary to present in this publication the specifications for the many standard pieces of equipment customarily used in libraries since that information appears in many sources. These would include charging desks, charging machines, catalog card cabinets, book trucks, atlas and dictionary stands, newspaper racks, office furniture, informal furniture, filing cabinets, adding machines, typewriters, cushions and hassocks for storytelling (in elementary schools), exhibit cases, and other equipment.

The items in the list that follows represent the additional equipment needed to meet the multimedia approach which good teaching and effective learning require from the school media program. Recommended quantities have been stated in two columns. The basic specifications indicate quantities needed for a functioning program, more traditional in nature. The advanced recommendations present quantities that will be needed in those schools with such instructional approaches as individualization of instruction and independent study. It is recognized that in certain types of innovative programs even the advanced level will need to be exceeded.

	Basic	*Advanced*
16mm sound projector	1 per 4 teaching stations plus 2 per media center	1 per 2 teaching stations plus 5 per media center
8mm projector (only equipment for which materials exist at the appropriate school level should be procured)	1 per 3 teaching stations plus 15 per media center	1 per teaching station plus 25 per media center
2×2 slide projector remotely controlled	1 per 5 teaching stations plus 2 per media center	1 per 3 teaching stations plus 5 per media center
Filmstrip or combination filmstrip-slide projector	1 per 3 teaching stations plus 1 per media center	1 per teaching station plus 4 per media center
Sound filmstrip projector	1 per 10 teaching stations plus 1 per media center	1 per 5 teaching stations plus 2 per media center
10×10 overhead projector	1 per teaching station plus 2 per media center	1 per teaching station plus 4 per media center
Opaque projector	1 per 25 teaching stations or 1 per floor in multi-floor buildings	1 per 15 teaching stations plus 2 per media center
Filmstrip viewer	1 per teaching station plus the equivalent of 1 per 2 teaching stations in media center in elementary schools and 1 per 3 teaching stations in media center in secondary schools	3 per teaching station plus the equivalent of 1 per teaching station in media center in elementary schools 3 per teaching station plus the equivalent of 1 per teaching station in media center in secondary schools
2×2 slide viewer	1 per 5 teaching stations plus 1 per media center	1 per teaching station plus 1 per media center

	Basic	Advanced
TV receiver (minimum 23 in. screen)	1 per teaching station and 1 per media center where programs are available	1 per 24 viewers if programs are available, in elementary schools 1 per 20 viewers in classroom, where programs are available, in secondary schools 1 per media center in both elementary and secondary schools
Microprojector	1 per 20 teaching stations	1 per 2 grade levels in elementary schools 1 per department where applicable in secondary schools 1 per media center
Record player	1 per teaching station, K-3 1 per grade level, 4-6 1 per 15 teaching stations in junior high and secondary schools 3 per media center 1 set of earphones for each player	1 per teaching station, K-6, plus 5 per media center 1 per 5 teaching stations plus 5 per media center in junior high and secondary schools 1 set of earphones for each player
Audio tape recorder	1 per 2 teaching stations in elementary schools plus 2 per media center 1 per 10 teaching stations in junior high and secondary schools plus 2 per media center 1 set of earphones for each recorder	1 per teaching station plus 10 per media center in elementary schools 1 per 5 teaching stations plus 10 per media center in secondary schools 1 set of earphones for each recorder

	Basic	*Advanced*
Listening station	A portable listening station with 6-10 sets of earphones at the ratio of 1 per 3 teaching stations	1 set of 6-10 earphones and listening equipment for each teaching station and media center
Projection cart	1 per portable piece of equipment, purchased at the time equipment is obtained	
Projection screen	1 permanently mounted screen per classroom plus additional screens of suitable size as needed for individual and small group use. The permanent screen should be no smaller than 70×70 with keystone eliminator.	
Closed-circuit television	All new construction should include provisions for installation at each teaching station and media center. Older buildings should be wired for closed-circuit television with initiation of such programs.	
Radio receiver (AM-FM)	1 per media center plus central distribution system (AM-FM)	3 per media center plus central distribution system (AM-FM)
Copying machine	1 per 30 teaching stations plus 1 per media center	1 per 20 teaching stations plus 1 per media center
Duplicating machine	1 per 30 teaching stations plus 1 per media center	1 per 20 teaching stations plus 1 per media center
Micro-reader (some with microfiche attachment)	Equivalent of 1 per 10 teaching stations to be located in the media center	Equivalent of 1 per 5 teaching stations to be located in the media center
Micro-reader printer	1 per media center	3 per media center

	Basic	Advanced
Portable video tape recorder system (including cameras)	1 per 15 teaching stations with a minimum of 2 recorders per building	1 per 5 teaching stations with a minimum of 2 recorders per building
Light control	Adequate light control in every classroom and media center to the extent that all types of projected media can be utilized effectively	
Local production equipment	Per building: Dry mount press and tacking iron Paper cutters Two types of transparency production equipment 16mm camera 8mm camera Rapid process camera Equipment for darkroom Spirit duplicator Primary typewriter Copy camera and stand Light box 35mm still camera Film rewind Film splicer (8mm and 16mm) Tape splicer Slide reproducer Mechanical lettering devices Portable chalkboard	

Items for special consideration	Large group instruction
	    The following equipment should be available for each large group instructional area:
	    10 × 10 overhead projector, auditorium type; large screen with keystone eliminator; 16mm	

projector, auditorium type
(consideration should be given to
the possible use of rear screen
projection)

Television

A complete distribution system
of at least six channels should
be available in a building so
that: broadcast TV 2500 MHZ,
UHF, or VHF can be received;
signals can be distributed to
each room from the central TV
reception area and/or from a
central studio; signals can be
fed into the system from any
classroom; signals are
available simultaneously

$3\frac{1}{4}\times4$ projectors

If still used by teachers at the
school building, there should be 1
per school building plus 1
auditorium type per each large
group instructional area.

Equipment to make tele-lecture
available

6

Supplemental services for the school media program

Effective media programs at the building level require supplementary services from media centers located in the headquarters of larger administrative units. Plans now in operation represent three levels of organization: the center for a school system or for a multi-school system arrangement, regional centers within a state, and the state center. System media centers furnish supervisory, advisory, coordinating, and other services of many kinds. The number of regional media centers, although small, is steadily increasing. All states provide some form of media services, and the majority have a formally organized office or center for this purpose.

Plans for some specialized supplementary services projected for the future include national and multi-state regional centers designed to provide a bibliographic apparatus for the evaluation, selection, and in depth analysis of materials, through the use of computer systems and electronic retrieval.

This chapter deals primarily with the system media center. Principles relating to services and staff, collections of materials, expenditures, and facilities are presented for system media programs. Quantitative standards are not indicated. Other sections deal briefly with regional media centers and the state media program.

System media centers

The recommendations in this section apply to media centers serving one or more school systems. Whether the system center is planned for a single school system or for several systems with contractual cooperative arrangements depends on the number of schools involved, size of student population, local policies, legal controls, geographical factors, and other considerations. Organizational plans for media centers providing services for more than one school system include: boards of cooperative services, the intermediate unit, the county district, mutual agreement contracts of less formally organized nature, and special projects funded by state and federal grants.

Large school systems generally maintain a single center; very large school systems may have branches of this center or their equivalent located in district offices within the system.

Regardless of the number of schools in a system, certain services (such as cataloging, technical processing, and advanced audiovisual production) should be provided by some central organizational unit. It is the responsibility of the officials of the school system to see that such services are made available and to determine which administrative arrangement results in the most educationally effective and economically sound plan. The programs of media centers in schools that have the availability of system media services under the direction of qualified media supervisors can provide students and teachers with a wider range of services and resources than would otherwise be possible.

Staff and services

A unified media program is desirable at the system level for the same reasons advanced for the unified media program at the building level (see Chapter 1).

The services provided by the system media program are represented in the following list of activities of the director of the system media center who, assisted by his staff:

Plans and develops media programs for the school system
Provides advisory services to the media specialists in the
    school buildings

Works with curriculum specialists and other school personnel in planning the instructional program of the school system

Arranges inservice programs for teachers, supervisors, and media center staffs in the use of materials and equipment

Serves as a resource consultant for district curriculum specialists

Participates in the meetings of professional staff members of the school district

Evaluates media programs at building and system levels

Interprets the media program to school administrators and the community

Submits proposals for innovative programs when feasible

Assumes responsibility for the formulation of materials selection policy for the school system

Makes provision for the evaluation of all materials; guides and coordinates the selection and acquisition of materials; assists in the selection of textbooks

Develops media budgets and supervises the expenditures

Manages the distribution, repair, and maintenance of equipment and resources

Determines staff requirements and participates in the selection of media center personnel

Supervises centralized processing of materials

Assumes responsibility for production of materials, television and radio programs, electronic banks of materials, and museum services, as well as study guides necessary for their proper and full utilization

Makes necessary preparations for media centers and programs in new schools

Serves as consultant for the school architect in designing the facilities for new centers, or in the renovation of existing facilities

Maintains liaison with other system supervisory staff and with state and national media personnel

Additional services provided by the director and his staff relating to resources are described in the following section on materials collections. (Responsibilities of the system center staff and of media specialists in the schools for the evaluation and selection of materials are described in Chapter 3.)

The director carries out the functions noted above with the assistance of a staff composed of media specialists, media technicians, and media aides.

Qualifications for professional personnel at the system level will require a higher degree of specialization than that indicated for media staff in the schools. It is desirable that competencies in the various curricular areas be represented by subject or other specialization among professional staff members. In view of the need to keep abreast of developments in the field and to provide specialized services, some specialization in form of media is also necessary, but this should not deter the broadly based media service.

In addition to the professional specialists needed to implement the system media program, the system media center will require a supportive staff of media aides, media technicians, and other personnel. It is emphasized, however, that staff in sufficient number and with a variety of competencies must be provided to accomplish the services of the system center as well as to furnish the backup services needed by the media center in the school. These services to the individual school include support in instructional matters, personnel, and budget; inservice education; evaluation, selection, production, processing and maintenance of materials; and special services (as for exceptional, physically handicapped, non-English-speaking, and other students). In the past, professional staff members of the system media center have had to devote most of their time to purely administrative, technical, and business matters. With a sufficient number of professional and supportive staff members, the system media specialists can assume in full degree their responsibilities as curriculum consultants, participants in planning and developing instructional and communications programs, and materials specialists.

Materials collections

Collections of resources that are available in the system media center include the following:

1. A collection of professional materials is provided for

teachers, media specialists, administrators, curriculum specialists, and other staff members in the school system for use in and circulation from the system center. The resources—consisting of books, periodicals, pamphlets, audiovisual materials, and copies of instructional materials (units of study, class projects, course outlines, and similar materials) developed in the local schools, in the state, or elsewhere—should be accessible after school hours, on Saturdays, and during vacation periods. The collection is larger than those provided in individual schools and does not obviate the need for working professional collections in the media center at the building level.

2. The system center has a collection of books and other resources needed by the staff of the district media center in connection with ongoing activities (for example: special tools used in technical processing and bibliographic and other sources for the acquisition of materials).

3. If the system media center offers supplementary reference services to the school media centers, the reference collection customarily found in the system center will have to be expanded in scope and depth.

4. Collections of periodicals beyond those customarily housed in the building media center can be made available through the system center. These would include current issues of scholarly, specialized, technical, or foreign magazines not subscribed to by the school media center. Available in microfilm would be back issues of these as well as of magazines and newspapers subscribed to by the school media center. System services that supply, in response to telephone or other forms of request, facsimile copies of magazine articles needed by teachers or students, are valuable if promptly executed, and if copyright laws are not violated.

5. The center should maintain collections of audio and video tapes intended for radio and television broadcast, transparency masters, collections of materials, models, dioramas, works of art, scientific apparatus, and other resources whose frequency of use does not warrant storage in the individual buildings.

6. The system center film collection must have a wide range of films easily accessible and with duplicate titles to meet de-

mands. Films are loaned to schools through the building media center. Rental of films may be handled by either the system or the school center, whichever can provide the fastest and most efficient service. Of prime importance is the immediate availability of the film when requested by the teachers. The expense of films is, in the final analysis, not as costly as the handicapping of the teachers' instructional plans when films are not available at the times needed.

7. The archives, housed in the system media center, include: annual reports, records, and similar documents; publicity items, files of school newspapers, magazines, yearbooks, and other publications; and material of an historical nature relating to the schools or school system served by the center.

8. Supplementary resources that are expensive, infrequently used, or highly specialized in nature can be made available in the system center for loan to school media centers for use by teachers and students.

9. The system center can act as a clearing house for interlibrary loans of materials from one school media center to another.

(10.) When financially feasible, the system maintains examination collections of trade books, textbooks, audiovisual resources, and other instructional materials suitable for children and young adults. These are usually titles which have been approved by selection committees and are made available to media specialists, teachers, and other personnel for examination before acquiring them for the school media center or before using them in instructional planning. Materials assembled for these examination purposes should be purchased, under most circumstances. Few system centers can or should afford collections extensive enough to meet the purpose for which these examination collections are intended, and consequently there is a need to develop larger organizational units for these resources.

Expenditures

Annual appropriations should be budgeted for the acquisition of materials for the collections of the system media center. The amount appropriated should be large enough to meet the current needs of the program of the system media center. To purchase collections for new media centers and to bring existing collections up to standard will require special allocations over and beyond the regular annual appropriation. Funds for the resources of the system media center are included in the expenditures recommended for the collections of media centers in the schools (see pages 35-37). These funds do not include school-adopted textbooks.

Funds, beyond those provided for materials, must be available for supplies and equipment, communications services, postage and shipping, delivery services, and offset printing.

Facilities

Considerable experimentation is underway in planning facilities for system media centers. Variations in local school organization and the relative newness of regional media centers within a state make it difficult to make precise recommendations for the system center at this stage. It is assumed that most electronic processing and also electronic media programing could be done at the regional level, but until these facilities are developed, the media program at the system level may have to make provision for them. Very large school systems are the equivalent of one or more of these larger organizational units.

The facilities of the system media center must be carefully planned to accommodate its program. Space and equipment are provided for the collections of materials and their related services, the media programs (television and radio, production of materials, and electronic systems), administrative and technical services, and staff activities.

Regional media centers

Regional media centers have been started in some states and are being projected in others. They have developed with a variety of administrative structures, a few functioning as arms or branches of the state media agency. Others derive from local initiative through the efforts of several cooperating school districts, often with the leadership of an intermediate unit of school administration, such as a county intermediate education agency, and are supported by combinations of local, state, and federal funds. Whatever the organizational pattern under which it is administered, the regional media center exists to provide services which smaller local school systems cannot easily provide for themselves.

Though services of regional media centers differ, in general they are similar to those provided by system centers in larger school systems. Often they include advisory, consultative and information services, technical processing, supplementary and special collections of resources, and a varied program of activities. Many regional centers include review and examination collections of instructional materials, selected professionally, and purchased for the use of both larger and smaller districts within the region. Some produce and provide educational radio and television programing, and serve as centers for computerized instruction, remote access materials, mobile units, and the like. Inservice education for teachers and media specialists is another important regional media center activity.

For very small school systems the regional media center is a substitute for the system media center; for larger districts it is supplemental and a source for some services which only the largest systems can supply for their own schools.

The state media program

Although variations exist among the states in number and size of schools and school districts, in geographic conditions, in socio-economic factors, and in the stages of development of media programs at all levels (school, system, and state), some basic principles are relevant for all state media programs.[1]

It is recommended that all states have directors (supervisors, coordinators, or equivalent term) of school library services and of audiovisual services. A comprehensive and coordinated media

1. For statements of policy see: Council of Chief State School Officers. *Responsibilities of State Departments of Education for School Library Services.* Washington, D.C.: The Council, 1961.

Council of Chief State School Officers. *State Department of Education Leadership in Developing the Use of New Educational Media.* Washington, D.C.: The Council, 1964.

program for the state is important if educational goals for the schools are to be fully met. This program may be achieved by a unified administrative organization or, with the proper controls and channels of cooperative planning and communication, by a coordinated administrative organization. It requires the planning of regional services designed for equalization of educational opportunity, maximum efficiency and economy, and avoidance of duplication of services.

The state media center forms an integral part of the state department of education or public instruction. This location assures the highest degree of participation by the director and staff of the media center in the development and improvement of media programs in schools within the state and facilitates the utilization of services available from the media center for curriculum specialists and other personnel in the department. Cooperation and coordination with the state library, museums, and television agencies are important. The state media center's primary responsibilities are with the schools and with other members of the state department working in the elementary and secondary school fields, and these can best be met when the center has membership in and close identification with that part of the structure of the state department of public instruction directly concerned with elementary and secondary education.

Index

(Note: "n" following a number indicates footnote on page.)

Centralized processing, 26, 53
Certification: educational, 13; study and evaluation of, 14; which allows for all variant patterns, 15. *See also* Professional education
Chalkboard, portable, 48
Circulation: and distribution, space requirements, 40; and loan regulations, 24
Classification scheme, 26
Classroom collections, 24-25
Clerical aide, *see* Media aide
Closed circuit television, *see* Television
Collections, *see* Basic collections of the media center; Classroom collections; Examination collections; Materials, professional; System media center
Commercial processing, 26
Communications center, xi. *See also* Media center
Computerized: instruction centers, 58; learning laboratory, space requirements, 43; programs of learning and instruction, 21
Computers: cataloging, use in, 26; use in projected supplementary services, 51
Conference rooms, space requirement, 41
Consultant: for school architect, 53; services, 4, 8
Copying machines, quantitative standards, 47
Copying services, policy for, 21
Curriculum: content, teacher involvement, 4; development and the media specialist, 3, 9; emphasis and the media program, 3; experimentation and expenditures, 36; innovations and selection of materials, 21; personnel and selection of materials, 21; planning, 8

Darkroom, space requirement, 42
Definitions, selected, xv-xvi. *See also* Terminology
Dictionaries, 25, 29
Dioramas, 15, 33, 55
District media center, 55
Dry mount press and tacking iron, 48
Duplicate copies, 21, 23, 34, 55
Duplicating machines, quantitative standards, 47

Education, professional, *see* Professional education
Educational process, the, 1-2
Educational programs, stressing individualization, 3
Electronic processing and electronic media programing, 57
Elementary schools: access to media center, 24; basic collections, 30, 32; media staff allocation in, 9
Encyclopedias, 25, 29
Entrance, space requirement, 40
Equipment, 4, 16, 23, 43-44; items for special consideration, 48-49; local production, 48; operation and maintenance, 16; quantitative standards, 45-49
Evaluation: and selection of materials, 20-22, 53, 54; and the system media program, 53, 54; of certification, 14; of materials, continuous process, 22
Examination collections, 56, 58
Exhibits, 15, 40
Expenditures for materials, 35-37, 56-57
Extended hours of service, 22-23

Facilities of media center: convenience, 24; designing and

Facilities of media center *(cont.)*
renovating, 53; environment, 39; equipment, general, 43-44; equipment, quantitative standards, 45-49; location and space, 39-40; resource centers or branches, 40; space for, quantitative standards, 40-43. *See also* Equipment; Space for media center facilities

Films: accessibility of, 23, 25; quantitative standards, 31, 31n; rental of, 56

Filmstrips: accessibility of, 23, 25; quantitative standards, 30

Funds, federal and state, 20, 58

Globes, in basic collection, quantitative standards, 32

Graphic materials, in basic collection, quantitative standards, 32

Graphics production and display, 15

Group projects and instruction in research, space requirement, 42

Hours of service, 22-23

Individual study and listening, space requirement, 41

Individual viewing and listening, space requirement, 40

Information services, space requirement, 41

Initial collections, funds for, 36, 57

Inservice education, 9, 11, 13, 53, 54, 58

Instructional materials center, xi. *See also* Media center

Instructional media center, xi. *See also* Media center

Instructional program, 3, 22, 35, 40, 53

Intermedia approach to materials, 2. *See also* Multimedia

Junior high school, basic collection of, quantitative standards, 30

Language laboratories, staff requirements for, 9, 16-17

Learning: process, 1, 2, 3; self-directed, 3; skills, 1

Learning resource centers, xi. *See also* Media center

Library media centers, xi. *See also* Media center

Light control, 48

Listening stations, quantitative standards, 47

Magazines: back issues, in microfilm, 55; facsimile copies of articles in, 55; in basic collections, quantitative standards, 30; in professional collections, quantitative standards, 33; in the classroom, 25; storage space, 42

Maintenance and repair service, space requirement, 42

Maps, in basic collections, quantitative standards, 32

Materials: accessibility of, 22-25; collections, 29-35, 54-56; expenditures for, 35-37, 56-57; organization of, 26-27; selection of, 20-22, 53. *See also* Materials, professional

Materials, professional: administration of, 34; center for, space requirements, 43; collections, quantitative standards, 33; in the system media center, 33, 54-55; itemized, 34; where housed, 35

Media: defined, xv; format of, 3; function in educational process, 1. *See also* individual kinds

Media aide: defined, xv; member, staff of system media center, 54;

member, supportive staff of media center, 15; paid by, 16; ratio to media specialists, 16, 17; services of, 16; volunteer assistance not equivalent of, 16

Media center: accessibility, 22-23, 24, 39; circulation and loan regulations, 24; class visits to, 24; collections, basic, 29-33; collections, professional, 33-35; defined, xi, xv; design, 24, 39; establishment of, x; expanded services and extended program, 22, 23, 24, 39; facilities, 39-49; in new school buildings, xii, 23, 53; instruction in use of, 8; location, 23, 39; resource centers of, 35, 40; resources of, 2, 22, 24, 29-35; schedules, staff, 23; space, quantitative standards, 40-43; staff, 7-17; supplemental services for, 51-59; textbook management in, 25. *See also* Media program; Media staff; Regional media center; State media program; System media center

Media production laboratory, space requirement, 42

Media program: administration of, 40; as resource for learning, 2-3; as resource for teaching, 3-4; defined, xi-xii, xv; elements of, 4; equipment for, quantitative standards, 43-49; importance of school board member to, 5; in new school building, xii, 53; in the school, 1-5; role in educational process, 1; space requirements for, 40-43; staff and services of, 7-17; supplemental services for 51-59; unified, philosophy of, 2; unified, recommended, 10. *See also* Materials; Materials, professional

Media specialist: allocation of, 9-10; at system level, 52-54; certification, 14-15; defined and explained, xi-xii, xv; education and preparation, 12-14, 54; needed in advance of new school opening, xii; ratio to students, 12; role in educational process, 1; role in selection of materials, 20-22; services and responsibilities, 2, 3, 7-10, 22, 25; status of, 7-8; work loads and schedules, 23

Media staff: allocation of, 9-10; at system level, 54; certification, 14-15; defined, xv; education and preparation, 12-14; head of, 10-12, 13, 25, 34, 40; professional, 7-15, 40; role in educational process, 1; scheduling, 23; supportive, of media center, 15-17, 40. *See also* Media aide; Media specialist; Media technician

Media technician: defined, xv; member, supportive staff, 15, 54; number and kind of, 15, 17; ratio to media specialists, 16-17; services, 15-16

Microfilm, 23, 44

Microform, in basic collection, 32

Micro-readers and micro-reader printers, quantitative standards, 47

Models, *see* Realia

Multimedia: approach, equipment required for, quantitative standards, 44-49; approach to materials, 2, 21; arrangement of materials, 26

Newspapers, 25, 55; in basic collection, quantitative standards, 30

Pamphlets, 34, 55; in basic collection, 30
Paperback books: as required textbooks, 25; encourage pleasure in reading, 23; for professional collection, 34; in the classroom, 25; large quantity in regular collection, 25; sale of in media centers, 25; widespread use of, 21
Periodical collections at system media center, 55. *See also* Basic collections; Materials, professional
Personnel, *see* Media staff
Photographic production, 16
Pictures and art prints, *see* Graphic materials
Print: and non-print materials, interfiled, 44; annual expenditures for, 35; specialization in, 13
Processing: centralized, 26, 53; commercial, 26; electronic, 57; information and materials, 15; technical, 52, 58
Production of materials, 3, 4, 8, 15, 48, 53
Professional collections, *see* Materials, professional
Professional education: and inservice programs, 13; development of unified program in colleges, 14; need for specialization, 12-13; needs review, 13; subject matter of, 12. *See also* Certification; Specialization
Professional materials for the faculty, *see* Materials, professional
Programed instructional materials, in basic collection, 33
Projection carts and screens, quantitative standards, 47
Projectors, quantitative standards: 8mm, 45; filmstrip or filmstrip-slide combination, 45; filmstrip, sound, 45; microprojector, 46; opaque, 45; 16mm, auditorium type, 48; 16mm sound, 45; slide, 2×2, 45; 10×10 auditorium type, 48; 10×10 overhead, 45; $3\frac{1}{2} \times 4$, 49

Quantitative standards: for basic collections, 29-33; for equipment, 45-49; for materials, professional, 33; for media center facilities, 40-43

Radio, space requirement, 43
Radio receivers (AM-FM), quantitative standards, 47
Reading and browsing area, space requirement, 40
Realia, in basic collection, 33
Recordings: accessibility of, 23; tape and disc, in basic collection, quantitative standards, 31
Record players, quantitative standards, 46
Regional media centers, 57-58; and centralized processing, 26; types of, 51
Remote access: materials, 58; programs, in basic collection, 33; staff requirements for, 9, 16-17; storage and control center, space requirement, 43
Resource centers, 35, 40. *See also* Facilities of media center

Schedules, work, 23
Scheduling, modular and flexible, 3, 24
School board: and innovative curriculum, 5; and selection policy, 20; employs media aides, 16; support for media program, 4, 5
School building or building level, references explained, xi
School librarian, *see* Media specialist

64

School libraries: and unified media programs, 2, 10; media center defined, xv; staff allocation during transition to unified center, 9; terminology related to, xi. *See also* Media center

Secondary schools: basic collections of, quantitative standards, 30, 32; media staff allocation in, 9

Selection of materials, *see* Evaluation: and selection of materials

Shelving, 41, 44

Skills, pupil, 1

Slides: in basic collection, quantitative standards, 32; 2 × 2 viewer, quantitative standards, 45

Small group viewing and listening area, space requirement, 41

Space for media center facilities, additional, 39-40

Space for media center facilities, optional, quantitative standards, 43

Space for media center facilities, quantitative standards: administration, 42; audiovisual equipment, distribution and storage, 43; center for professional materials for faculty, 43; circulation and distribution, 40; conference rooms, 41; dark room, 42; entrance, 40; group projects and instruction in research, 42; individual study and learning, 41; individual viewing and listening, 40; information services, 41; magazine storage, 42; maintenance and repair service, 42; materials and equipment storage for production, 42; media production laboratory, 42; reading and browsing, 40; small group viewing and listening, 41; stacks,

42; storytelling (elementary schools), 41; workroom, 42

Specialization, professional: kinds of, 13, 54; need for, 12-13; of first and second professionals, 11; required of system center personnel, 54

Splicers, film (8mm and 16mm) and tape, 48

Stacks, space requirement, 42

Staff, *see* Media staff

Standards for school media programs: application, xii, xiii; functions of, x; in new schools, xii; national, compared with state and regional, x-xi; purpose of, ix-xi; revisions, x-xi; scope, xii-xiii; terminology explained, xi-xii. *See also* Definitions

State department of education or public instruction, 59

State media program, 58-59; staff specialization, 13; supplementary services, 51

Storage, space requirements for: audiovisual equipment, 43; magazines, 42; materials and equipment for production, 42; remote access, 43; television properties, 43

Storytelling area, space requirement, 41

Student assistants, 16

Supplemental services for media program: levels of organization, 51; regional media centers, 57-58; state media program, 58-59; system media centers, 52-57

System media center: activities of director, 52-53; and regional center, 58; defined, xi, xvi; expenditures, 56-57; facilities, 57; materials collections, 54-56; organization of, 52; selection policy of, 20; services, 51-56;

System media center *(cont.)*
staff, 54; unified program for, 52

Teachers: and educational process, 1; and locally produced materials, 22; and media program, 2-4, 8-9; and selection of materials, 21
Teaching station defined, xvi
Technical processing, *see* Processing; Cataloging
Technician, *see* Media technician
Television: closed circuit, 9, 47; outlets, 41; receivers, 46; staff, 9, 16-17; storage, 43; studio, 43; systems, 49; video tape recordings, 33, 44, 55
Terminology of the standards, xi-xii. *See also* Definitions

Textbooks, 25, 29
Transparencies, 15, 44; in basic collection, quantitative standards, 33

Unified media program: at system media center, 52; defined, xvi; development of, 10; intermedia or multimedia approach of, 2; philosophy of, 2. *See also* Media program

Video tape recorder systems, quantitative standards, 48
Video tape recordings, *see* Television
Viewers, filmstrip and 2×2 slide, quantitative standards, 45

Workroom, space requirement, 42